Partners In Healing

The Ministry Of Anointing

From the Library of
Janice Kulp Long
&
John R. Long

Frank Ramirez

CSS Publishing Company, Inc., Lima, Ohio

PARTNERS IN HEALING

Copyright © 2005 by
CSS Publishing Company, Inc.
Lima, Ohio

All rights reserved. No part of this publication may be reproduced in any manner whatsoever without the prior permission of the publisher, except in the case of brief quotations embodied in critical articles and reviews. Inquiries should be addressed to: Permissions, CSS Publishing Company, Inc., P.O. Box 4503, Lima, Ohio 45802-4503.

Scripture quotations are from the New Revised Standard Version of the Bible, copyright 1989 by the Division of Christian Education of the National Council of the Churches of Christ in the USA. Used by permission.

Scripture quotations marked (KJV) are from the King James Version of the Bible, in the public domain.

Library of Congress Cataloging-in-Publication Data

Ramirez, Frank, 1954-
Partners in healing : the ministry of anointing / Frank Ramirez.
   p. cm.
ISBN 0-7880-2378-0 (perfect bound : alk. paper)
1. Unction. 2. Spiritual healing. 3. Church of the Brethren—Liturgy. I. Title.

BX7825.5.U53R36 2005
265'.7—dc22

2005015361

For more information about CSS Publishing Company resources, visit our website at www.csspub.com or e-mail us at custserv@csspub.com or call (800) 241-4056.

Cover design by Luke Scasny/Phil Eriksen
ISBN 0-7880-2378-0   PRINTED IN U.S.A.

Dedicated to Phil Franklin, along with Mike and Merry Titus. In 1972 we worked together in the dish room at La Verne College. What better way to find a church home?

Table Of Contents

Introduction	7
The Ministry Of Anointing	11
Introduction To The Ordinance	11
A Ministry Of Healing	12
Some Thoughts On Healing	16
The Place Of Forgiveness	17
The Power Of The Community's Prayer	18
The Laying On Of Hands	18
Invitation To Anointing	19
Preparation Of The Individual For Anointing	21
Other Situations	22
The Physical Elements Of Anointing	23
A Basic Service Of Anointing	25
Other Services Of Anointing	29
In Times Of Emergency	29
In Times Of Confession	29
Historic Anointing Services	31
From An 1887 Church Manual	31
From The 1942 Book, *The Office Of Deacon: Manual Of Instructions*	31
A Hymn For Anointing	35
Scriptures And Prayers For Use During Anointing	37
The Lord's Prayer — Matthew 6:9-13 (KJV)	37
Psalm 23 (KJV)	37
Prayer For Divorced People	38
Prayer In Time Of Crisis	38
Prayer For Nightfall	39
Prayer During Difficult Times	39

Prayer During Financial Distress	39
Prayer To Settle Disagreements	40
Prayer Of Praise	40
Prayer During Time Of National Distress	40
Prayer During Wartime	41
Prayer Of Thanksgiving	41
Prayer For Glory	41
Prayer For Perfection	42
Prayer For Fulfillment	42
A Call For Forgiveness	42
Sermons	**45**
Lights, Camera, Action	45
Anointing For Healing	49
Meditations	**53**
Eureka!	53
You Anoint My Head With Oil	54
Discussion Questions On Anointing For Study Groups	**57**
Additional Questions Regarding The Laying On Of Hands And Public Prayer	**59**
Experiential Exercises	**61**
Children's Activity	**63**
Brethren Resources	**65**

Introduction

How very good and pleasant it is when kindred live together in unity! It is like the precious oil on the head, running down upon the beard, on the beard of Aaron, running down over the collar of his robes. It is like the dew of Hermon, which falls on the mountains of Zion. For there the Lord ordained his blessing, life forevermore. — Psalm 133

I'm old enough, I suspect, that at some point in my childhood I used what they called "greasy kid stuff" to keep my hair in place. However, that very phrase insured that I would abandon the stuff for a drier look when I got older.

We don't dump olive oil on our heads in order to refresh ourselves. However, there is something about the abandon of this psalm, the idea of allowing the stuff to drip down the beard and around the clothes, that invites us into a more trusting and less controlling relationship with God.

In our own society it is in victory that we allow ourselves to lose control. The players dump a huge container of ice and sticky sweet drink over the coach in the last moments of the game. Players spray themselves with champagne even though it stings the eyes and stains the clothes.

But the victory of Jesus over life and death doesn't always elicit the same hollering and high jinks. Many want worship to be an experience in which emotions and actions are kept firmly under control. Children are kept quiet, either in some distant nursery or behind a glass wall that is largely sound proof, or under the baleful stares of their elders. Worshipers rise to their feet but only for a quick and furtive trip to the restroom. Hymns are limited to three or four stanzas and the stomachs of worshipers provide a check to any call from a chorister for another rousing chorus.

Anointing for healing is a biblical ordinance that recognizes that God is firmly in control of all aspects of our lives. It is our invitation to God to re-enter our lives through doors we may have closed. It is a reminder that all healing resides with the Spirit of

God. It is a comfort that God cares for us and desires wholeness, shalom, healing, for the people of God.

Anointing for healing is not a last rite (although I have anointed people on death's door as they prepared for the ultimate healing and restoration), and it is little practiced. My people, the Church of the Brethren, celebrate anointing for healing as part of their attempt to restore a New Testament church. Of course, in our brokenness we have been as successful and unsuccessful as everyone else. Indeed, for part of the twentieth century we slipped away from our classic understanding of the ordinance, and thus required an effort to restore it to its proper place. I have discovered in my 25 years of ministry that anointing for healing is an essential rite, and a blessed time to be shared with those who are ill, their families and friends, and on occasion, the whole family of God.

Anointing for healing, rather than being a last rite, is for those who are sick physically, emotionally, or spiritually. The rite is intended for wholeness as well as curing. It is performed at homes, in hospitals, and in worship. Built around James 5:13-15, it does not command God, but invites God to take part in the healing process. Some (including myself) can point to cases of miraculous cures. Others point to feelings of wholeness, wellness, even in the midst of illness.

Anointing for healing is not a substitute for medical care by licensed physicians, nurses, and technicians. God's Spirit is working with us, through us, despite us, around us. In some cases where I have offered anointing in hospitals, the medical personnel have remained with the patient to be anointed, as well.

The purpose of this little book is not to suggest that those who have not practiced this ordinance, or have practiced it in a different way, are in any way deficient. It is to share what has blessed us even as we seek to listen and learn from our sisters and brothers in fellow communions. There is one church, one body of Christ, and if at this time we share in his body as diverse fellowships, then at the least we can make lemonade out of lemons by blessing each other with what we have learned on the road to Emmaus. Jesus has been in our midst, and on those occasions when we recognized the fact, we ought to say something about it.

Some years ago, I wrote another book for CSS Publishing Company on the ordinance of feetwashing and the Love Feast titled *He Took A Towel*. As was the case with that book, I have included the biblical and historical background to the ordinance of anointing for healing, as well as some sample services and prayers, and concluded with a couple of sermons for use in introducing the ordinance to congregations. In addition, I have included some discussion questions for those who might use this book for small group study.

Frank Ramirez

The Ministry Of Anointing

Are any among you suffering? They should pray. Are any cheerful? They should sing songs of praise. Are any among you sick? They should call for the elders of the church and have them pray over them, anointing them with oil in the name of the Lord. The prayer of faith will save the sick, and the Lord will raise them up; and anyone who has committed sins will be forgiven. Therefore confess your sins to one another, and pray for one another, so that you may be healed. The prayer of the righteous is powerful and effective.
— James 5:13-16

Introduction To The Ordinance

I take anointing personally, and seriously. I'll never forget the time back in 1979 when Francisco, our first son, was born. We were a month from graduation at Bethany Theological Seminary, when Cisco was born three months early. After a difficult birth that nearly killed his mother, he struggled for life as a premature infant, hovering near death. About five days after he was born, two professors from the seminary, Donald Miller and Nancy Faus, representing the community of faith, came to us and performed an anointing. For both of his parents and for him, the event became a turning point. Healing entered our frightened lives, and for Cisco it was the beginning of a cure.

A couple of years later, my wife, Jennie, was expecting again and the pregnancy went bad. She was confined to bed. One Sunday, however, she struggled to church for an anointing administered by my fellow minister, Nolan Porter. Six months later, my daughter, Jessica, was born as healthy as could be.

Anointing has been an essential part of my ministry. On some occasions anointing followed the alarming results of medical tests. Further tests would reveal nothing was wrong at all. There have been situations where an anointing for a sister or brother on death's door seems to have been a signal that God had called them forth from death's door back into healthy life. There was the anointing for a woman who'd lived a full life and was ready to slip away.

Anointing eased her passage. I remember a man who'd grown weary of the endless barrage of medical procedures for a bad heart. After an anointing, his heart catheterization showed he was perfectly clear. He lived a year free of medical procedures, then died quickly, the way he preferred.

I have been anointed, as well. At my ordination, or at my installation as pastor of various churches, I have been anointed. When I faced difficulties in my life as a pastor I have sought anointing for wisdom and peace of mind.

Many of the anointings over which I have officiated have been for peace of mind, for wholeness, for calm. Some of the prayers at the heart of the anointing have been answered. Others were not answered as I wished, but God has always answered prayer faithfully. There have been out-and-out miracles. There have been miracles of grace.

A Ministry Of Healing

Anointing for healing is one of the essential rites of the church. The scriptural case for the ordinance is strong, contained in the direct command of James 5:13-16. The ministry of anointing is consistent with the call in scripture for petitionary prayer.

In one of the final scenes of the movie, *The Wizard of Oz*, the title character is whisked away in his balloon by accident while Dorothy calls frantically from below for him to come back. "I can't!" he calls back, admitting, "I don't know how it works!"

When it comes to petitionary prayer I have to admit I don't know how it works and I don't know why it works. That's an essential mystery of our relationship with God. If God already knows what we want and if we confess that God knows far better than us what it is we need, then praying for something seems not only unnecessary but even untrusting. Should we not just trust God to do what is best for us?

But, for whatever reason, God has called us to pray, and not simply to pray, but to pray for what we want. In the Lord's Prayer we not only praise God's name and pray for God's will to be done, but we also pray for our daily bread, to be forgiven, and to be strengthened against temptation.

A good parent often knows what a child not only needs, but what a child wants even before being asked, but there is something special about the asking that strengthens a relationship and allows for a closer walk.

Our life of prayer, along with obedience, service, and discipleship, strengthens our relationship with God, and that relationship is a crucial aspect of our faith. The God revealed in the Bible is a God who covenants with us, who has a history with us. When Moses wants to know who is speaking out of the burning bush, the reply comes, "I am the God of your father, the God of Abraham, the God of Isaac, and the God of Jacob" (Exodus 3:6). It is by calling to mind God's history of relationship that we know God.

I like the way my friend and fellow pastor, Scott Duffey, puts it. "From God's promise to make Abraham into a great nation, to Jesus' personal sacrifice on the cross, God has always been at work in people's lives reconciling, healing, sustaining, and redeeming. The rites and ordinances of the church are all about these activities of God, and our responses."

What is the biblical warrant for anointing? In the Old Testament, anointing with oil was part of the rite that set apart kings. It was not for everyone. The title of Messiah which we assign to Jesus means "the anointed one," the one set aside as the descendant of King David.

But there is one reference at least, in Leviticus 14:14-18, in which the priest is instructed to anoint a leper with oil prior to cleansing. When Jeremiah asks, "Is there no balm in Gilead? Is there no physician there? Why, then, has the health of my poor people not been restored?" (Jeremiah 8:22), one may assume that the balm, or oil, was used by a physician in healing.

An essential element of the New Testament is that we are now considered part of the royal family! In Galatians 4:1-7, for instance, Paul writes that just as heirs "as long as they are minors, are no better than slaves," so, too, we, though slaves to our past, are now adopted into God's family. So intimate is that relationship that we should refer to God as "Abba," the Aramaic word not for "father" but for "daddy" or "da-da." As Paul concludes, "So you are no longer a slave but a child, and if a child, then also an heir, through God."

One of God's desires for the people is that they should be one. In the ancient world sickness meant separation from the community. The Old Testament law provides rules for separating the sick from the community at large. Becoming sick meant becoming an outsider, just at the time when we need the support of family and friends the most.

The ministry of healing that Jesus practiced in the gospels is more than a ministry of curing. Cures took place, but the important thing was that individuals were restored to their families and friends. These miracles pointed to God's coming kingdom, and how all will be restored in time, but the community of faith seeks now to include rather than exclude, to restore those who have taken ill, or who are disabled, or who might be considered pariahs in other societies or circumstances, back into our midst.

Jesus set an example in sending out his disciples into ministry to their fellow believers. "So they went out and proclaimed that all should repent. They cast out many demons, and anointed with oil many who were sick and cured them" (Mark 6:12-13).

Jesus, the anointed one, seems to have invited all to be anointed. Because of his saving ministry we have no need of mediators, so the practice of anointing is for everyone, not just those in positions of leadership or authority.

First John 2:20 and 27 refer to the anointing experienced by all believers, as does Paul when he writes in 2 Corinthians 1:21 "But it is God who establishes us with you in Christ and has anointed us...."

The primary passage for the ordinance is, of course, James 5:13-16:

> *Are any among you suffering? They should pray. Are any cheerful? They should sing songs of praise. Are any among you sick? They should call for the elders of the church and have them pray over them, anointing them with oil in the name of the Lord. The prayer of faith will save the sick, and the Lord will raise them up; and anyone who has committed sins will be forgiven. Therefore confess your sins to one another,*

and pray for one another, so that you may be healed. The prayer of the righteous is powerful and effective.

The text calls for all to be involved. The believer should pray on his or her own behalf. That person should also call upon the community of faith to join in prayer, specifically inviting elders, however that may be interpreted, to pray. Though our society seems to encourage us to be loners, taking care of ourselves without any help, the biblical model is one of mutual aid and care. "We do not live to ourselves, and we do not die to ourselves" (Romans 14:7-8).

Back in 1708, when a small group of believers met together in Bible study to reconstruct the early church, they determined that the text from James clearly required the group to practice anointing among themselves. Not only was the biblical opportunity clear, but these believers also searched the ancient church fathers, and found confirmation for the practice there, as well.

There is plenty of evidence about the use of anointing for healing in the life of the early church. In *The Apostolic Tradition: A Commentary*, the authors trace early church practice through the manuals preserved in several languages. There is an assumption that the ministry of healing will be practiced by the church[1] and it includes the following prayer for the consecrating of healing oil:

> *Send, Lord, the richness of your mercy upon this fruit of the oil, through which you anointed priests, prophets, kings, and also martyrs, and clothed in kindness with the garment of your righteousness, in order that for everyone coming for anointing it may be for advantage and benefit of soul and body (and) spirit, for averting of every evil, for health to the one anointed through our Lord Jesus.*[2]

Among the other early writers who refer to this ministry of healing are Origen, Irenaeus, Justin Martyr, Chrysostom, and Hippolytus of Rome.

Some Thoughts On Healing

All healing comes from God. There are occasions when miraculous healing occurs which defies medical explanation. However, it seems to please God to work through humans as well, even though, without doubt, God could do a better job. Nurses, doctors, and technicians of all stripes aid in the healing process, and their skill, the result of long years of training in most cases, has its roots in the gifts of God.

There are several kinds of healing. Physical healing is the most dramatic and often the most desired form of healing. But there are times when emotional, spiritual, or psychological healing is just as important as physical healing.

Healing is a gift and not a right. The prayer of faith is powerful, but the most faithful prayer of power was that of Jesus in the garden of Gethsemane, on the eve of his great ordeal: "Father, if you are willing, remove this cup from me; yet, not my will but yours be done" (Luke 22:42). Anointing cannot guarantee healing. If it could it would border on magic, and would imply that we in some way control God's actions. God is in control of history and healing. It is God who invites us to join into a community of prayer through the ordinance of anointing.

Anointing affirms our partnership with God, a partnership necessary for true healing to take place. It begins with God, from whom restoration and healing has its source, and includes the wider church, from the spiritual leaders through the believer who feels alienated or ill. God forgives, saves, and loves us. The Body of Christ, the church, seeks to embody this embracing and inclusive love through the ministry of prayer and anointing.

The prayer of faith can save us. The means and matter of that salvation, from cure through healing, restoration to earthly health, or redemption into eternal health, are up to God.

If the result prayed for does not occur it is not an indication of a lack of belief or faithfulness on the part of anyone who participated. It is expected that God will act freely and may not be constrained or coerced, and that in answering, God may choose in the negative as well as the positive.

Healing at its best represents a holding action. Death is the birthright of every human being, with extraordinarily rare exceptions. Enoch and Elijah are the only ones that come to mind. Healing is most effective when it becomes a gateway into a richer quality of life, and a return to discipleship.

Some make a distinction between healing and curing. One of the elements of anointing is prayer for the forgiveness of sins. Wholeness, shalom, can be the response of God toward every petition, regardless what happens physically to those who pray. Those who participate in anointing need to be open to an unexpected and unexplainable manifestation of God's grace. Anyone who has participated in many anointings becomes aware that miracles happen at the time and place of God's choosing, and that God continues to act directly in history, as well as working through individuals.

In my tradition we do not consider anointing a last rite. However, this should not be used as a reason to deny those near death the comfort which is afforded by the service. Those who have chosen to be anointed during the difficult times in their lives may wish to be anointed in the final crisis as well. In addition, because some may consider death as a friend and not an enemy, there may be occasions when suffering could be relieved by God's calling a believer home. Easing that path in accordance with God's will is an acceptable desire through anointing, and the service recognizes that the choice rests with God.

In all of these ways, God's Spirit is moving among us as we challenge each other to remain open to that Spirit. God does long for our wholeness and health, and James has provided us a means to seek after it. May we seek the Lord wherever he may be found.

The Place Of Forgiveness

Great emphasis is placed in our society on feeling well, of living pain-free. Little attention is paid to the importance of restoring and maintaining relationships with God and with each other. We often remember in the well-known story of Jesus and the paralytic that the man with the long-term illness was cured, and that certainly is a cause for rejoicing. But when the man was first lowered through the roof Jesus said, "Son, your sins are forgiven" (Mark 2:6).

The religious authorities found it hard to deal with the fact that Jesus forgave sins, in some ways more than the fact that Jesus healed and cured. The forgiveness of sins and the restoration of relationships can have a far more lasting effect for a believer than simply curing ailments.

As will be seen below, the invitation to anointing is also an invitation to forgive and be forgiven, by God and by each other. This aspect of the ordinance should not be ignored. In the Lord's Prayer we pray, "Forgive us our debts, as we forgive our debtors." It's not a case of cause and effect. Our works, in this case forgiving others, do not save us. Rather the state of righteousness which God established at the beginning of time, and which is the aim of the prophets and the Revelator, calls all of us to restore and be restored.

The Power Of The Community's Prayer

The community of prayer is recognized as a powerful gift to God's people. In the book of Daniel, Shadrach, Meshach, and Abednego gather with Daniel to form a community of prayer in the face of oppression and while waiting for God's guidance. God's people gather in the upper room following the crucifixion, and later the resurrection, and pray. It was to the gathered community that the Spirit was first given at Pentecost. There is a constant exhortation to prayer in the letters of Paul. Prayer is available to all people and there is no requirement that prayer be performed in a particular way, outside of the guidance of the Lord's Prayer. Nevertheless, it strengthens God's people if they pray together.

The Laying On Of Hands

One of the essential components of the anointing service is the laying on of hands. This is generally administered following the administration of the anointing oil, and consists of one of those officiating laying both hands upon the head of the person who is anointed. Others participating might place their hands on the officiant's hands.

Physical contact during healing was a part of the ministry of Jesus. Although he healed at a distance on more than one occasion, Jesus touched some of those who were healed (see Matthew 9:18; Luke 4:40; Mark 16:18; Acts 9:12, 17). In many cases those who were ill also became social outcasts. The laying on of hands in the anointing service is important if for no other reason than for the opportunity to reach out and touch those who need healing. We act as did Jesus.

In addition, there is precedent in scripture for the laying on of hands during acts of blessing (Genesis 48:14-19), dedication (Numbers 8:10), and the blessing of children (Matthew 19:13, 15). The laying on of hands is also used during baptism (Acts 8:17, 19; 19:6) and the installation of officials (Acts 6:6; 13:3; 1 Timothy 4:14; 2 Timothy 1:6).

Although James 5:3-16 makes no reference to its use during the anointing service, a passage from "Against Heresies," a second-century tract by Iraenaeus makes reference to the practice, as do many other passages among the early church fathers.

As is the case with the rite of anointing, we do not believe the action of laying on of hands insures that physical healing or the desired answer to a prayer will occur in all cases just because the action has been performed. Nor does something magical occur just because of the use of hands. However, this symbolic act represents the gift of the Spirit that is the common property of God's people. To quote *The Brethren Encyclopedia*: "Those who impose hands are agents of God and represent the imparting of God's love, blessing, and power."

Invitation To Anointing

Although there may be, in some churches, an unspoken invitation for anointing, it is better if ministers and elders or deacons remind individuals in times of physical, spiritual, and emotional crisis that anointing is available through the community of believers. This can be done by bringing the possibility of anointing to the attention of those who may need it, as well requesting the ordinance for themselves.

One of the best ways to support the ministry of anointing is for church leaders to take special care to utilize the ordinance themselves, and to make it a part of the worship service. Although it is certainly appropriate for the anointing to take place in the home and in the hospital, when the rite takes place in the worship service it offers the entire congregation the chance to minister, and demonstrates the anointing service to those who may have little or no acquaintance with it. Church leaders can model the special blessings available in a church anointing by requesting it themselves prior to surgery or anticipation of crises, or during crises. In these instances the one officiating the service may invite the one who is to be anointed to kneel or sit in the front of the sanctuary. Church leaders and others who have a special interest in the case should join the one to be anointed (and indeed the entire congregation may come forward depending on the physical layout of the area).

During the laying on of hands the leaders may place a hand on the officiant's hands, or on the shoulders of the one being anointed or the officiant. Others may put a hand on the shoulders of those closest, until everyone in the congregation is in contact with someone else.

In addition to modeling the benefits of the anointing service for others, stories may be used to demonstrate the value of anointing. The newsletter might feature testimony from those in the congregation who have experienced physical or emotional healing through anointing. The pastor may be encouraged to feature anointing as a message or series of messages.

Finally, church leaders who are actively involved in the lives of the members of the congregation may recognize situations in which an anointing may be helpful. There should be no coercion in matters of religion, so some sensitivity should be used in the invitation. Care should be taken so that the visit or conversation does not seem intrusive to the person involved.

Typically, the leader should speak with the suffering individual about the situation itself, exhibiting concern. At some point in the conversation the deacon might say, "Have you considered an anointing?" or "Are you familiar with the rite of anointing?"

If the individual expresses interest, the leader might explain a little about the practice, and ask, "Would you like me to call the pastor to arrange an anointing?" or "Would you like to be anointed?"

It may be that the individual will be wary or worried about anointing. In that case the sensitive church leader or pastor should seek other ways in which the congregation can minister.

Church leaders who are actively involved in the lives of members will find it easy to bring up the possibility of anointing.

Preparation Of The Individual For Anointing

Just as important as the actual anointing is the preparation for anointing. Those taking part in the anointing should be actively involved in the preparation.

Anointing may take place in the home, in the hospital, in the church, or at the scene of the crisis. In many cases, circumstances will be relatively calm. It is important to be sensitive to the suffering person's condition. Extreme pain can mean relatively short spans of attention. Unusual emotional suffering may make it difficult for the individual to concentrate.

The pastor may arrange, for instance, for the anointing to take place at the home of the individual to be anointed. In that case the service will take on the appearance of a visit, as well. It is important to ask after the health and well-being of all individuals, and even to invite spouses and others present to be anointed, also. Care should be taken to put everyone at ease. Small talk is an appropriate entrance to more serious matters.

An opportunity should be given to the sufferer to confess any anxieties, worries, or sins that might be troubling that person. Leaders may offer to help bring about any reconciliation that might be standing in the way.

The person can be gently encouraged to discuss the exact nature of the illness or trouble, too. It is important for deacons to hear what the individual is saying, and not read their own agenda into these statements. Although some comfort might be taken from others who have had the same experience, it is not always necessary to say, "The same thing happened to me." On the other hand, the stories of those who have endured similar trials may be helpful, as long as they are not used as guarantees of a successful outcome.

Pastors and others must take care to hear the seriousness of the illness or trouble. To simply say, "It will be all right," or "Everything will be okay," trivializes the situation. It is important that the anointing not be used as a "quick fix" designed to minimize the suffering or put an end to the congregation's activity. It is an invitation to a closer relationship with God and the congregation.

At some point, the actual service should be described. After the description of the service, care should be taken so that the sufferer is seated or laying in a comfortable position. The service, selected from those listed on pages 25-43, follows.

Afterward, if the anointing takes place at the home, care should be taken for the ministry team to depart with sensitivity. If the anointing is at the hospital, shortly before surgery, some members of the caring team should prepare to remain with family members during the operation.

Other Situations

Although the point might be made that young children cannot fully appreciate the meaning of the anointing service, it is better to include children and accept their level of understanding. Children are often excluded from the mainstream of the congregational life, and relegated to second-class status.

In addition, the peace and comfort extended to parents, grandparents, or guardians makes the service worthwhile, even if the children involved are infants and have no understanding of the service.

In any event, God is capable of responding to prayer, regardless of the understanding of a particular child.

The same things are true in those instances when the person to be anointed is unconscious. First of all, it is not always certain that a person who appears unconscious is not comprehending at some level. In addition, comfort can be extended to family members and God is able to respond in any event.

The Physical Elements Of Anointing

It may seem obvious, but it is essential to have some sort of oil for anointing. To that end it is good to have a small vial or container that is clean and easy to maintain and transports easily.

The very first anointing I observed while a student minister was at a morning worship service. The service involved the entire church and was very moving. Later, the minister told me he'd forgotten his vial of oil and had gone downstairs to the church kitchen and found some Crisco shortening.

For people in some traditions, such as my own, the actual substance used is not as important as it might be to others. We believe God alone is holy. However, you should use materials appropriate to your own traditions.

Many denominations have some sort of container of oil available for purchase. Sometimes this is more of a petroleum jelly in a small, flat disk. Other times it is a liquid oil in a vial.

To be honest, I tend to take the small, sample-size bottles of Tabasco sauce and after emptying them I soak them, removing the label and all traces of residue. I fill the bottles with olive oil, and leave one in my car, one in the pulpit, one in my office, and others around where they might prove useful. These seal well and can be placed in a pocket.

When I have totally forgotten my oil and found myself in circumstances where oil is not easily obtainable, such as a hospital, I have improvised. At hospitals, for instance it is usually possible to speak to a nurse and get a small foil of Vaseline, which works just as well.

---

1. Paul F. Bradshaw, Maxwell E. Johnson, and L. Edward Phillips, *The Apostolic Tradition: A Commentary*, edited by Harold W. Attridge (Fortress Press, Minneapolis, 2002), p. 81.

2. *Ibid.*, p. 51.

A Basic Service Of Anointing

(Share a time of visitation and prayer as previously outlined. At the appropriate moment begin the service by saying the following words.)

In a moment we will share in the ordinance of anointing. I will read aloud from scripture. I will anoint our brother/sister with oil for the forgiveness of sins, the healing of the body, and the restoration of wholeness to the soul. If anyone else would like to be anointed at this time please tell me.

Following the anointing I will lay my hands on our sister/brother's head. I invite you all to either place your hands on mine, or to place your hand on my shoulder or another's shoulders, so that we are gathered together in touch as well as in heart. I will pray aloud. When I cease my spoken prayer I will remain silent. During that time I invite anyone who feels led to pray aloud to do so. If you feel led to pray silently, please do so. Do not be afraid of silence. Do not feel you must pray in order to fill the silence. Silence is very powerful. When I feel that all have prayed aloud who would like to, I will conclude with a short prayer and the Lord's Prayer. I invite you to join me in the Lord's Prayer.

(Open the Bible and read aloud Lamentations 3:19-24 and/or James 5:13-16.)

> *The thought of my affliction and my homelessness is wormwood and gall! My soul continually thinks of it and is bowed down within me. But this I call to mind, and therefore I have hope: The steadfast love of the Lord never ceases, his mercies never come to an end; they are new every morning; great is your faithfulness. "The Lord is my portion," says my soul, "therefore I will hope in him."* — Lamentations 3:19-24

> *Are any among you suffering? They should pray. Are any cheerful? They should sing songs of praise. Are any among you sick? They should call for the elders of*

> *the church and have them pray over them, anointing them with oil in the name of the Lord. The prayer of faith will save the sick, and the Lord will raise them up; and anyone who has committed sins will be forgiven. Therefore confess your sins to one another, and pray for one another, so that you may be healed. The prayer of the righteous is powerful and effective.*
> — James 5:13-16

We are gathered together to anoint our *(brother/sister)* in the presence of God for *(give reason for anointing)*. We come together boldly and with courage because Jesus commanded us to pray "Give us this day our daily bread." We come meekly with the fears of Jesus when he prayed, "Not my will, but thine." Knowing that in the midst of a broken world God wills your wholeness in body, mind, and spirit, I now anoint you with oil —

(The leader places a few drops of oil on a finger and anoints the forehead with oil in the shape of three crosses. There are a variety of ways to handle the oil. It can be used directly from a bottle, or a small amount can be poured out into your hand. From this source, touch your fingers to the oil and then touch the person's forehead, and repeat it three times, once with each petition listed above.)

— for the forgiveness of your sins, the granting of peace to your soul, and the restoration of wholeness to your body.

(The leader will then lay hands on the head, one on top of the other, of the one being anointed. Others present may lay their hands upon the leader's, or upon a shoulder, until all are touching. The leader may pray extemporaneously, or something along these lines. The prayer may vary greatly depending on the circumstance, for example, if the service is shared before surgery, during a long illness, at a time of crisis, and so forth.)

Lord of healing, God of glory, we know that no matter where our journey may take us, you are already there, waiting to bless us, waiting to embrace us. We believe that your will for our lives includes wholeness, shalom, forgiveness, health. We also know that we live in a broken world, and that for a time we suffer as you suffered.

If it is your will we pray boldly that you will heal our brother/sister, restoring him/her to health, drawing us all closer together in your name. We pray you will guide the hands of your healers, doctors, nurses, technicians, and others who are partners with you for healing. We pray for wisdom and discernment, clear diagnosis, and healing for all present.

Most of all, though we have come boldly before the throne of grace to present our petition, we pray with your Son and our Savior Jesus Christ the same words he pronounced at the Garden of Gethsemane, when he begged that the cup might pass from him, not our will, but your will be done.

Trusting in your mercy, your wisdom, your glory and power, trusting in your will for our lives, we continue to pray.

(After the leader's prayer a silence follows in which others may pray aloud or silently as they choose. The leader closes with a brief spoken prayer, followed by the Lord's Prayer in which all may join in.)

Lord, we offer up to you all our prayers, spoken and unspoken, trusting in your goodness and mercy, as we pray together the prayer of your Son and our Savior, saying together in one voice, "Our Father, who art in heaven, hallowed be thy name. Thy kingdom come, thy will be done on earth as it is in heaven. Give us this day our daily bread, and forgive us our debts, as we forgive our debtors, and lead us not into temptation, but deliver us from evil: For thine is the kingdom, the power, and the glory, for ever. Amen."

(In both public and private worship it may be appropriate to sing before and after the service. Here are some suggested hymns.)

"Great Is Thy Faithfulness"
"There Is A Balm In Gilead"
"In The Bulb There Is A Flower"
"Amazing Grace"

Other Services Of Anointing

In Times Of Emergency
(On those occasions where there is no time for preparation a single sentence may have to suffice.)

"_____, I anoint you with oil for the healing of your body, the forgiveness of your sins, and the restoration of wholeness to your soul."

In Times Of Confession
(Anointing presents an opportunity for the person being anointed to offer his/her personal confession, or to give a testimony to their faith. A traditional way of saying it is:)

"As far as you know, are you at peace with God, or is there anything in your life that you believe might prevent you from receiving the full blessing of God? Are there any thoughts or feelings you'd like to share?"

(Pause and let them contemplate and share. Don't be afraid of silence. Don't be in a hurry. After they have shared you might ask:)

"Is there anything else you'd like to share?"

(Assure them of God's forgiveness. Follow the sharing with words of reassurance of God's love and grace. Remember, God can forgive those things that are too deep even for words if we approach God with a repentant heart. Say something like:)

"God is faithful and just and will forgive us our sins at any time when we turn to God with repentant hearts. May this loving God now bless us through this service."

(Anointing)

Upon your confession and affirmation of faith before God and these people, I now anoint you with oil in the name of Jesus
- for the forgiveness of your sins,
- for the strengthening of your faith,
- and for healing and wholeness according to God's grace and wisdom.

(Laying on of hands and prayer)

(After the third anointing, lightly place your hands on the head of the person being anointed. If there is a group of people present, they can surround the person and join hands, with persons on either end laying a hand on the anointed person. Each deacon is invited to pray briefly. Others in the group may pray aloud, too. When all are finished, everyone closes with the Lord's Prayer.)

(Benediction and Departure)

"May the God of hope fill you with all joy and peace in believing, so that you may abound in hope by the power of the Holy Spirit. Amen."

(All may offer hugs and signs of personal support before leaving.)

Historic Anointing Services

From An 1887 Church Manual

As regards the anointing, it requires two brethren to perform it according to the advice of the apostle, since he says: "Let them call for the elders of the church, and let them pray over him." These words require more than one. Now, when we are going to perform the same, the first thing we do, after singing a few appropriate lines and briefly exhorting, is to turn to God unitedly, and to pray to God for a blessing upon ourselves, upon the sick member, and upon all as we do in a meeting, and there is liberty to pray for all the brethren present. If time will permit, and strangers are present, the passage from James 5 may be read, as far as relates to this matter, and briefly commented upon. Then the sick member is raised to a sitting posture, and the elder brother reaches for his hand, and the other brother pours the oil upon it, which he, the first, puts upon the head of the sick, and thus three times saying the words of the apostle: "Thou art anointed in the name of the Lord, unto the strengthening of thy faith, unto the comforting of thy conscience, and unto a full assurance of the remission of thy sins," or as the Lord may give utterance; and then the brethren both put up their hands on the sick, even as it is done when a brother is ordained, and pray chiefly for the sick member. Such an example we have of the Savior, as we see in Mark 6:13 and 16:18, and this is the order the brethren have administered the same. Brethren, also, who are not ordained may administer it in case of necessity.

From The 1942 Book,
The Office Of Deacon: Manual Of Instructions

... If conditions are favorable, a suitable hymn may be sung. Following this a brief prayer of consecration should be offered. Then one of the brethren should read from James 5:7-18. Opportunity may be given for explanations or questions on the scripture. Following this, a brief examination may be given, such as:

"Are you willing to commit your case completely into the hands of the Lord as the great physician of your body as well as your soul?"

"Are you willing to confess and forsake every sin you may have committed that his grace may not be hindered?"

"So far as you know, are you at peace with God and our fellow men? Is there any hindrance that might prevent you from entering into the fullness of the blessing he holds for you at this time?"

Then follows the anointing service.

"Dear brother (or sister), upon thy confession of faith and thy willingness to commit thy case into the hands of God, thou art anointed with oil in the name of the Lord, for the strengthening of thy faith, for the forgiveness of thy sins, and for the healing of thy body."

The brother who assists should pour out a few drops of oil in the palm of the brother who officiates, as he repeats each part of the formula with "for," who in turn puts it on the head of the patient. After applying the oil, both brethren lay their hands on the head of the patient, and each in turn offers a short prayer on behalf of the patient, committing the case to the hands of the Lord.

Anointing Prayer For A Dying Person

At this time we ask for God's mercy and grace to be made evident in death as well as life. Recognizing that in each end is a beginning, and placing full trust in the risen Lord who said to a sinner, "Today you will be with me in paradise," I anoint you with oil for the forgiveness of sins, for clarity of mind and intent, and the restoration of wholeness to your soul.

Let us pray. Dear God, we offer to you this life which was yours from the beginning, and which is now given back to you, the Lord of life. We pray boldly for miracles, for wholeness and healing, and at the same time we pray for the strength to echo your son in the Garden of Gethsemane, as we pray, "Not my will, but thine." If it is your will that your servant and our brother/sister is to be called from this life we ask that you give us the gift of the peace that passes understanding to all present, and to all loved ones both near and far. Let your servant go in peace, for our eyes have seen your salvation in the person of Jesus Christ our Lord, who taught us the words that we now pray — "Our Father, who art in heaven, hallowed be thy name, thy kingdom come. Thy will be done on earth as it is in heaven. Give us this day our daily bread, and forgive us our debts, as we forgive our debtors. And lead us not into temptation, but deliver us from evil: For thine is the kingdom, and the power, and the glory, for ever. Amen" (Matthew 6:9-13 KJV).

A Hymn For Anointing
To the tune Hyfrydol ("Come Thou Long-Expected Jesus")

(Note: Although the third stanza was written for the Advent season, the hymn can be used in all seasons, with or without the final verse.)

Come, God's people, be anointed,
Claim God's healing balm at last.
Set aside your pride and passion,
Christ has fully paid the cost.
All that's fleeting, all that's passing,
Has its day, then fading,
But your healing is forever,
Lasting past the final day.

Come, God's people, claim God's pleasure,
Joys await to those who heed.
Nothing for the self-sufficient,
Everything to those in need.
Come now forward, as if limping,
Gladly lean so burdens bear,
Small and great, all harms are healing,
If we have a tear to share.

Go, God's people, forth with treasure,
Not with gold or silver weighed.
With the lamp to light dark places,
With the truth that cannot be swayed.
From the manger comes the healer,
Who upon the cross in scorn
Bore our wounds and brought salvation,
Born to us on Christmas morn.

Scriptures And Prayers For Use During Anointing

As brothers and sisters, we come together to pray for our Christian brother/sister during a time of dread and suffering. We pray first for the healing of your Holy Spirit, that the powers of body, mind, and spirit be restored. We pray that the light of Christ will shine in his/her life more brightly because of his/her commitment to obedience to your commands, as seen by the desire to partake of your goodness through this service. We pray for patience as we wait for your action in his/her life. We pray as well the prayer of Jesus — not our will, but yours — as in obedience to his words we pray with the words which your Son and our Savior taught us, saying in one voice:

The Lord's Prayer — Matthew 6:9-13 (KJV)

Our Father which art in heaven, Hallowed be thy name.
Thy kingdom come. Thy will be done in earth, as [it is] in heaven.
Give us this day our daily bread.
And forgive us our debts, as we forgive our debtors.
And lead us not into temptation, but deliver us from evil: For thine
    is the kingdom, and the power, and the glory, for ever. Amen.

Psalm 23 (KJV)

The Lord is my shepherd; I shall not want.
He maketh me to lie down in green pastures: he leadeth me beside
    the still waters.
He restoreth my soul: he leadeth me in the paths of righteousness
    for his name's sake.
Yea, though I walk through the valley of the shadow of death, I
    will fear no evil: for thou [art] with me; thy rod and thy staff
    they comfort me.
Thou preparest a table before me in the presence of mine enemies:
    thou anointest my head with oil; my cup runneth over.
Surely goodness and mercy shall follow me all the days of my
    life: and I will dwell in the house of the Lord for ever.

Heavenly Father, we pray that you will watch over our brother/sister during this time of trial. We pray boldly for healing, for restoration to wholeness. We ask for calmness and peace. We pray first of all that you will heal directly in the body through the action of the Holy Spirit. We believe also you work through the hands of the healers. We pray that you will guide the hands of the doctors, nurses, technicians, and others involved in this surgery. Watch over friends and family both near and far. These things we pray in your Son's name. Amen.

Prayer For Divorced People

Lord it is not your will that the least of your servants should stumble. It is not your will that those who make a solemn choice should part. Nevertheless we know that all have sinned and fallen short of the glory of God. Now we ask that where there is brokenness, there might be healing. Where there is despair, there might be hope. Help us to be the instruments of your peace. Help us to be the church for people who are hurting. Help those who are hurting to remember that you are there with them. We know that life is filled with little deaths and little resurrections. It is so hard to see ahead to the time when healing may have taken place. Bless now your servant who desires to be healed. Bless now this person, who is one of your children, whose life is full of turmoil and doubt and despair. Bring light into the dark places of his/her life and hope in the middle of this troubled life.

Preserve, too, all those involved in this brokenness, all those whose lives are touched by disarray and difficulty. Teach them that your love is constant, fill them with the sense of your presence, bind their wounds and carry them through the tough days that lie ahead. These things we pray in your Son's name. Amen.

Prayer In Time Of Crisis

Dear Lord, rarely have we felt so confused, so harmed by life, so much in need of your love. Be by us now during a time when there seems to be no solution, no answer, only questions. Let your word be our light as we walk through dark places. Let your Spirit be our guide as we walk through the valley of the shadow of death. Let your Son be our example as we tread uncharted regions of the soul. Let your creation be our assurance, even as everything falls apart around us, that summer and winter, springtime and harvest, will not cease.

These things we pray in your Son's name. Amen.

Prayer For Nightfall

God of light, God of truth, abide with us as evening falls. The stars shine bright, and you gave them their light. The trees are silvered, and it is you who dress them with the light of the moon. The world is transformed, and yet it is still your earth, your sky, your sea. We are grateful that there is no place we can go that you are not already there. Be with us now as your people as we gather together in your name. Amen.

Prayer During Difficult Times

Lord, we know you are present, but we don't share the sense of your presence. Help us to feel that you are walking close beside us during this difficult time. As you led your people through the desert with a pillar of fire by night and a pillar of cloud by day, help us to see clearly the markers you have placed in our lives, so we may follow you through the dry places of discipleship, and on to the promised land of your kingdom. In Jesus' name we pray. Amen.

Prayer During Financial Distress

Loving God, we have seen the example of your Son in the multiplication of the loaves and fishes. We know there is enough and more for us to share, that all may be satisfied. You called for your disciples to aid Jesus in that miracle and you call for us again to call plenty into being again. Help us to become your presence in this world, fulfilling the physical as well as spiritual needs of those in our community as well as around the world. These things we pray in your Son's name. Amen.

Prayer To Settle Disagreements

Jesus, as we struggle through disagreements help us to recall that we are all your people, that you have called us into one family, that you are not interested in our squabbles. Help the promise that at your name every knee will bow, as we come together in unity based on your lordship and not our power. Your disciples asked to sit at your right hand, and we ask that that we might prove as worthy if we will seek to be your servants first and foremost. Bless us with the peace that passes understanding. In your name we pray. Amen.

Prayer Of Praise

God, there is no other but you, no desire as great as the desire to serve you and see you, no longing so deep as the longing in our hearts to be with you and abide by you, no joy so profound except the joy that comes from true apprehension of your works, and no satisfaction greater than when we praise your name. When I recall the works of your hands, in the lives of our ancestors in the faith and in the days of our generation, I proclaim that you are a living God who visits your people in every age, a caring God whose love is felt intimately from the rising to the setting sun, and a saving God, who in the darkest night of our lives abides with us though fast falls the eventide. I will praise you daily, and should I forget to praise, then I beg you to recall to my mind my pledge to you. In Jesus' name we pray. Amen.

Prayer During Time Of National Distress

Holy, holy, holy, Lord God almighty, who are we, a people of unclean lips living in a world of nucleons, to glimpse your glory even from afar in the faces of the human family. Nevertheless we cry aloud, as if fueled by your will, "Here we are! Send us!" Send us into the midst of a tortured land to proclaim the day of your salvation. Send us into a broken people to proclaim that in Christ there is no east or west, in Christ no south or north. Send us through a confused nation to demonstrate through your steadfast love that there is neither black nor white, Asian or Hispanic, native or immigrant, but one people called to the city of God, the pure bride of

Christ, descending from the clouds to live in the midst of God's people. You are Lord, and we are your followers. Fill us with your power not for our gain but for the fulfillment of your will. This we pray in your strength. Amen.

Prayer During Wartime

Lord, as nations again feel called to war, as men and women seek to settle their differences through the might of arms, give us the courage to witness now as in the past, that you are the Prince of Peace, that you favor no side, that you love all individuals. You do not know nations or aims or causes. You know us by our name and not by our citizenship. You are not on anyone's side. It is your desire that all come to the cross and stand by your side. If you will give us the strength, we will be your witness while passions are strong and reason is weak, calling all again to favor peace and abandon war. Amen.

Prayer Of Thanksgiving

God, this is your world, not ours. We thank you for quiet gardens, the first tomato of the season, the abundant zucchinis in paper sacks. We thank you for fertile fields, abundant corn, waving grain. Accept our offering to you, which we bring before you, with the resolve that what is yours is only temporarily ours. Let us be worthy in our sharing of this gift you have given to us. Thank you, thank you, thank you, for the renewal of your promise that until the end of time, summer and winter, springtime and harvest, will not cease. Amen.

Prayer For Glory

Lord, we pray now for the return of your Son and our Savior. We know that Jesus will come at a time of your choosing and not ours, and we will continue to wait patiently as your servants Simeon and Anna. Nevertheless, we reveal to you our heart's desire, that even as we pray your Son will return, that all will confess that Jesus Christ is Lord, that what we have known in part will be known by all, in full. We see through a glass, darkly. We desire to see you face to face. If it is your will that we wait a little longer, we accept this, but it is our desire to say as God's people, "Now let your servant depart in peace, for our eyes have seen the glory." We pray in expectation of that glorious day. Maran Atha. Come, Lord Jesus. Even so. Amen.

Prayer For Perfection

Lord, what have we forgotten to do? What have we neglected? Who have we ignored? Open our eyes that we may see, open our hearts that we may love, open our ears that we may hear. Let your will become ours. Perfect us in your love. Amen.

Prayer For Fulfillment

Lord of life, these autumn winds cause leaves to fall, and wake us to the coming of the cold. This is the time of watching signs, departing birds, receding dreams. We know what we wished to do and what we have not accomplished. We call to mind completed tasks. We catalog regrets and carefully shelve for future days those intentions we have fulfilled. All times are yours and all needs you fulfill in their season. Thank you God for the animals in their burrows, preparing for deep winters' sleep, and for the life of your people, waiting to be fulfilled in Christ. Lord of lords, God, Light of light, true God of true God. You are what you are. We are your people. This we pray in your Son's name. Amen.

A Call For Forgiveness

Forgiving God, we pray this day for those condemned to die. Whether or not they have committed crimes which shock or grieve us, we acknowledge you as Lord of life and death, and affirm that vengeance is yours, not ours. We call to mind as well the pain and sorrow of family and friends who have lost dear ones as a result of violence, and ask you to comfort survivors even as you have sheltered those who died in pain. What we cannot undo we give to you. What we can change you give to us. Hear our prayer, in our confusion. Fulfill our desire to be your will in a world of ambiguities. Deliver us from darkness and dark desires. Let the least of your children come to you in this hour. For we are convinced that nothing is beyond your forgiving love, and that neither life, nor death, nor angels, nor rulers, nor things present, nor things to come, nor powers, nor height, nor depth, nor any other created things will be able to separate us from the love of God which is in Christ Jesus our Lord. Amen.

Sermons

Lights, Camera, Action
Luke 8:40-56 and James 5:13-16

One of the more successful dramatic techniques is to get the audience involved in an important story, and just when it seems the story is reaching a climax, to cut away to another compelling story. At first you almost resent the breakaway, but then you get so involved that you hardly remember the first story, until you return to it!

Luke uses this sandwich technique to tell the story of double healings in the ministry of Jesus, and at the heart of the story is the compassion Jesus has for those who are suffering.

The opening verses *are* compelling. It's crowded, which seems to be usual when Jesus comes to town, and a leader from the local synagogue has a need so great he falls at Jesus' feet. His daughter, approaching a marriageable age, is dying. He needs Jesus and he needs Jesus right now.

We might miss something important because of our own vantage point in the twenty-first century, so I'd better spell it out. This is a daughter that is dying. In many cultures and in many times daughters are simply not valued as highly as sons. Women were not considered as valuable as men.

But the evangelist Luke, in both his Gospel and the Acts of the Apostles, emphasizes the place of women in the ministry of Jesus. Their monetary and spiritual support of the ministry of Jesus, their prominent place as ministers and teachers during the time of the apostles, and their ability to make salvation decisions without being tied to a husband or father, is markedly different from the other New Testament sources.

A daughter is worth saving, as far as Jesus is concerned. That's part of the ministry of compassion. Daughters are worth as much as sons. Jesus leaves immediately to take care of her.

Nothing happens in a vacuum. A woman "who had been suffering from hemorrhages for twelve years" seeks his aid, as well.

Since Jesus was in a rush he ought to have continued without taking any notice of this woman, and he certainly shouldn't have healed her to reward her impudence. But Jesus acts out of compassion, not calculation.

Luke tells us that she had spent all of her money and found no relief. Certainly many of us can share her frustration, considering the high price of health care, and the difficulty some people have in having their ailments properly diagnosed.

Just as crucial as her illness, with all the discomfort and feelings of shame that might have gone with it, is the fact that by the very nature of her condition she is unclean. Unclean, that is, by the standards of her society. Unclean means that she is not worthy to be touched or even approached. She must be sequestered, kept separate from the support systems of family, friends, and the faith community just at the time when they matter most.

In contemporary terms, there are illnesses or conditions that cause people to feel they are unworthy as well. Rather than catalog these and perpetuate the myth that some are unapproachable, I'll use one example, the obvious one of HIV/AIDS. Over the course of the last couple of decades there has been a recognition that it is possible, with the right drug therapies and a few precautions, for people with HIV/AIDS to live relatively normal lives. It wasn't that long ago that the stigma attached was so strong that threats to life and limb followed the revelation that one had the disease, regardless of the manner in which one contracted the condition.

It was only when prominent individuals made a point of visiting folks with HIV/AIDS, and also touching them, holding hands, comforting them and receiving comfort, that the barriers for at least some people were broken down.

In South Africa, for instance, where the condition is particularly prevalent, some began to wear T-shirts proclaiming they had the disease, even when they personally did not have it. These actions were intended to break down the walls the society had erected between those who had and those who did not have HIV/AIDS.

Back to the story — the woman did not feel worthy to approach Jesus, and acting out of tremendous faith decided to surreptitiously touch "the fringe of his clothes." This, by itself, was a barrier-breaking action, since women and men who were not married had no contact in that society.

The woman is immediately healed by the contact, but in order, I think, to make it clear that no magic is involved, Jesus establishes a relationship with the woman. He refers to her as daughter, despite the fact that anyone who had spent twelve years seeking a cure might well have been close to his own age.

Many times people think that prayer or religious ordinances consist of saying the right words in the right order and performing the right actions in the right manner. It's not. It's about having a relationship with Jesus. That relationship is founded in faith, so Jesus said, "Daughter, your faith has made you well; go in peace."

Go in shalom, or wholeness.

There's always too much to do. The fact that Jesus stops to create a relationship with the sick woman means that he's too late — the little girl is dead. And death, among the people of God, was the ultimate unclean condition. Those who meant to take part in religious services had to have someone else take care of their dead, or else they would disqualify themselves from temple worship for a time.

Just as he was not afraid to be touched by the unclean woman, Jesus is also not afraid of walking into the unclean place of death. From this story, I conclude the fact that just because someone has died does not mean it is too late for Jesus to save them. Being dead does not mean you're beyond the love of Jesus.

"Only believe and she will be saved," Jesus tells the anxious father. This mirrors the faith displayed by the sick woman. A return to life is a return to community. Jesus tells the family to feed the daughter, because the bread we break is at the heart of our relationship.

Ezekiel, in the vision of the dry bones, was asked, "Can these bones live?" It turned out they could. We who follow Jesus are taken to unclean places, and we see that quality of life and healing can take place.

It is precisely because healing is an essential wish that we are extending a call to all who wish to join us in the ordinance of anointing for healing, praying with those who are suffering because we believe (and observe) healing that takes place miraculously through the Spirit, as well as through the near miraculous intervention of doctors, nurses, and other health professionals. When we pray the prayer of faith we cannot demand that a cure take place. That would be magic, a belief that our actions control a god. Instead, we must believe that it can happen, demonstrating a relationship with God through our beliefs.

We pray boldly not only for what we wish, but for what God desires. Because even when there isn't a cure, there can be healing, wholeness, shalom, and there is always room for compassion.

Since God can heal us when God chooses, some may wonder why we need to have this service. Well, we don't need it at all, but God seems to us to be our partner in healing. God seems to desire us to ask, and this service calls for us to act, to give, and to receive; it calls us to state our desires before God and the community.

In the letter of James we read the following words: "Are any among you suffering? They should pray. Are any cheerful? They should sing songs of praise. Are any among you sick? They should call for the elders of the church and have them pray over them, anointing them with oil in the name of the Lord. The prayer of faith will save the sick, and the Lord will raise them up; and anyone who has committed sins will be forgiven. Therefore confess your sins to one another, and pray for one another, so that you may be healed. The prayer of the righteous is powerful and effective."

And in Mark, chapter 6, verse 13, we read that at the instruction of Jesus the disciples "... cast out many demons, and anointed with oil many who were sick and cured them."

Christians throughout history have anointed each other for healing. The Bible gives us clear instructions for being a partner with God in healing. This partnership includes doctors, nurses, medical technicians, friends, family members, and everyone else concerned with the health of an individual, but at the heart of this partnership is God, the source of life and salvation.

Following this message we will invite all who desire to come forward for anointing. However, if you wish to be anointed in private, in your home, at a hospital before surgery, or in the church office, you may privately make such a request, also.

God is faithful and just. God is present. It is time for us to be present with God, as well.

Anointing For Healing
James 5:13-16 and Lamentations 3:19-24
(The following sermon is built around the opening pages of this book.)

In one of the final scenes of the movie, *The Wizard of Oz*, the title character is whisked away in his balloon by accident while Dorothy calls frantically from below for him to come down. "I can't!" he calls back, admitting, "I don't know how it works!"

When it comes to petitionary prayer I have to admit I don't know how it works and I don't know why it works. That's an essential mystery of our relationship with God. If God already knows what we want and if we confess that God knows far better than us what it is we need, then praying for something seems not only unnecessary but even untrusting. Should we not just trust God to do what is best for us?

However, for whatever reason, God has called us to pray, and not simply to pray, but to pray for what we want. In the Lord's Prayer we not only praise God's name and pray for God's will to be done, but we also pray for our daily bread, to be forgiven, and to be strengthened against temptation.

A good parent often knows what a child not only needs, but what a child wants even before being asked, but there is something special about the asking that strengthens a relationship and allows for a closer walk.

Anointing for healing is part of that closer walk. In the Old Testament, anointing with oil was part of the rite that set apart kings. It was not for everyone. The title of Messiah which we assign to Jesus means "the anointed one," the one set aside as the descendant of King David.

In the New Testament, we are now all considered part of the royal family! In Galatians 4:1-7, for instance, Paul writes that just as heirs "as long as they are minors, are no better than slaves," so, too, we, though slaves to our past, are now adopted into God's family. So intimate is that relationship that we should refer to God as "Abba," the Aramaic word not for "father" but for "daddy" or "da-da." As Paul concludes, "So you are no longer a slave but a child, and if a child then also an heir, through God."

One of God's desires for the people is that they should be one. In the ancient world sickness meant separation from the community. The Old Testament law provides rules for separating the sick from the community at large. Becoming sick meant becoming an outsider, just at the time when we need the support of family and friends the most.

The ministry of healing that Jesus practiced in the gospels is more than a ministry of curing. Cures took place, but the important thing was that individuals were restored to their families and friends. These miracles pointed to God's coming kingdom, and how all will be restored in time, but the community of faith seeks now to include rather than exclude, to restore those who have taken ill, or who are disabled, or who might be considered pariahs in other societies or circumstances, back into our midst.

Jesus set an example in sending out his disciples into ministry to their fellow believers. "So they went out and proclaimed that all should repent. They cast out many demons, and anointed with oil many who were sick and cured them" (Mark 6:12-13).

Jesus, the anointed one, seems to have invited all to be anointed. Because of his saving ministry we have no need of mediators, so the practice of anointing is for everyone, not just those in positions of leadership or authority.

The primary passage for the ordinance is, of course, James 5:13-16:

> *Are any among you suffering? They should pray. Are any cheerful? They should sing songs of praise. Are any among you sick? They should call for the elders of the church and have them pray over them, anointing them with oil in the name of the Lord. The prayer of faith will save the sick, and the Lord will raise them up; and anyone who has committed sins will be forgiven. Therefore confess your sins to one another, and pray for one another, so that you may be healed. The prayer of the righteous is powerful and effective.*

The text calls for all to be involved. The believer should pray on his or her own behalf. That person should also call upon the community of faith to join in prayer, specifically inviting elders, however that may be interpreted, to pray. Though our society seems to encourage us to be loners, taking care of ourselves without any help, the biblical model is one of mutual aid and care. "We do not live to ourselves, and we do not die to ourselves" (Romans 14:7-8).

All healing comes from God. There are occasions when miraculous healing occurs which defies medical explanation. However, it seems to please God to work through humans as well, even though, without doubt, God could do a better job. Nurses, doctors, and technicians of all stripes aid in the healing process, and their skill, the result of long years of training in most cases, has its roots in the gifts of God.

There are several kinds of healing. Physical healing is the most dramatic and often the most desired form of healing. But there are times when emotional, spiritual, or psychological healing is just as important as physical healing.

Healing is a gift and not a right. The prayer of faith is powerful, but the most faithful prayer of power was that of Jesus in the Garden of Gethsemane, on the eve of his great ordeal: "Father, if you are willing, remove this cup from me; yet, not my will but yours be done" (Luke 22:42). Anointing cannot guarantee healing. If it could it would border on magic, and would imply that we in some way control God's actions. God is in control of history and healing. It is God who invites us to join into a community of prayer through the ordinance of anointing.

Anointing affirms our partnership with God, a partnership necessary for true healing to take place. It begins with God, from whom restoration and healing has its source, and includes the wider church, from the spiritual leaders through the believer who feels alienated or ill. God forgives, saves, and loves us. The body of Christ, the church, seeks to embody this embracing and inclusive love through the ministry of prayer and anointing.

The prayer of faith can save us. The means and matter of that salvation, from cure through healing, restoration to earthly health or redemption into eternal health, are up to God.

This means that if the result prayed for does not occur it is not an indication of a lack of belief or faithfulness on the part of anyone who participated. It is expected that God will act freely and may not be constrained or coerced, and that in answering God may choose in the negative as well as the positive.

Some make a distinction between healing and curing. One of the elements of anointing is prayer for the forgiveness of sins. Wholeness, shalom, can be the response of God toward every petition, regardless what happens physically to those who pray. Those who participate in anointing need to be open to an unexpected and unexplainable manifestation of God's grace. Anyone who has participated in many anointings becomes aware that miracles happen at the time and place of God's choosing, and that God continues to act directly in history, as well as working through individuals.

In all of these ways, God's Spirit is moving among us as we challenge each other to remain open to that Spirit. God does long for our wholeness and health, and James has provided us a means to seek after it. May we seek the Lord wherever he may be found.

Meditations

Eureka!

(Read Isaiah 9:2-7 and James 5:13-16.)

According to the Greek historians, Archimedes had a tough mathematical problem. A king had asked him to determine if a crown he had been given was pure gold or if it contained other base metals. Of course, if Archimedes had melted it down he would have known the exact percentage of gold and alloy, but that would have destroyed the crown.

Stumped, Archimedes went to the public baths and settled into the hot water to think. As he did so, he displaced the water and some of it spilled over. Suddenly, Archimedes had what we call a "light bulb moment." Gold had a certain weight and displaced water a certain amount, and other metals which had a different weight displaced different levels of water. Using a piece of gold the same weight as the crown as a test he should be able to determine the amount of gold in the crown.

He was so excited he jumped up naked and ran through the town shouting, "Eureka!" which is Greek for "I found it!"

There are a couple of light bulb moments involved in this passage. The first flash goes to those who first heard Isaiah and realized that in the coronation of a king (possibly Hezekiah who ruled from 715-687 B.C.) there was hope even in a desperate political situation. Later, God's people saw the light of Christ and realized that these verses also pointed ahead to the King of kings.

Our response to finding God, whether in a verse, or in our lives, should be to run out shouting, "Eureka!" and "We found it!" although I recommend we skip the bath and the running naked through the town part. Go out and tell others. Come and see.

One of the exciting things discovered in this verse is that the king is many things: Wonderful Counselor, Mighty God, Everlasting Father, Prince of Peace. Sometimes we say God is the ruler of our lives, but we act as if God had no part to play in our day-to-day lives. The king is not only the ruler, but also the healer.

If we truly accept God as not only Lord of our lives, but the leader of our day-to-day existence, then we have truly experienced a light bulb moment, and should shout, "Eureka!" The life God calls us to is one of wholeness and shalom even in the midst of travail, and that crown which God has promised us is pure gold.

You Anoint My Head With Oil
(Read Psalm 23 and Revelation 7:9-17.)

Once I traveled to Guatemala with a church delegation. We came to a courtyard in which the names of all those killed in a bloody civil war — the innocents who were murdered, assassinated, slaughtered — were carved into columns.

I couldn't help but look for my own last name, and there it was, several times. I knew that some of those people had been cruelly tortured before they were killed. Others were murdered in front of their families. I also knew that some of their murderers still walked the streets, worked in the government, perhaps even sat securely in the halls of justice. But the names on the columns are a stark reminder that God's justice will be served and that these people are not forgotten. There is a God who balances the scales.

John the Revelator gives us a look into heaven and shows us the people who gave their lives, who bled red, but are now fed at the wedding feast of the Lamb. They will hunger no more, thirst no more, suffer no more. They have triumphed.

The scene itself is part of a pause in the action of Revelation, a reminder that there is still time for us to take the side of the Lamb who bears the marks of slaughter, and who is our shepherd, having borne our sorrows and shared our grief.

We who are still suffering look to a shepherd to guide us, the Lamb who is our shepherd, who knows our infirmities, because he has lived them. This is no ivory tower God, but the real deal, who got his hands dirty, even bloody.

The world is filled with suffering. In our church every family is broken. Every family has troubles. There is one who loves us the way we are, desires our healing, and desires the healing of the nations. In the passage from Revelation, we get a glimpse into heaven filled with multitudes of those who once suffered, but are now at peace, and rejoicing.

In Psalm 23, we are told about a perfect shepherd who leads us beside the still waters, who restores our souls — and who anoints us with oil. The anointing is for the healing of the nations, but also for us as individuals, as well. Once anointing was reserved only for kings and rulers, but now, through Christ, we are all part of the family of the king. We are all royalty. We are all called to be anointed.

There are overwhelming numbers in the kingdom now, each with their own crown. Our healing is just a matter of time. The Lamb is our shepherd, not only over there, but right here and now. The Lord is my shepherd, not the Lord will be or someday might be my shepherd — *is*.

In this pause we have time to accept the mercies of the shepherd. We have the opportunity to be anointed, for our own healing and for the healing of the nations. Though we walk through the valley of the shadow of death we will fear no evil. God is with us. Amen.

Discussion Questions On Anointing For Study Groups

1. Read the text from James 5:13-16 aloud. If you had no prior experience with the anointing service, what assumptions would you make about the ordinance?

2. Share with the group instances in which you yourself have been anointed, if any. What were the circumstances? What prompted you to seek anointing? Did you have the idea, or did someone else? What were you praying for? What was the outcome? Would you recommend anointing for others?

3. Share with the group instances in which you were a participant in an anointing, not the person who was being anointed. How did it come about that you became involved? What were your feelings about the event?

4. What meaning do you give to the words "cure" and "heal"? Is there a difference, in your opinion?

5. What is the significance of anointing for your congregation? Do you think it is overemphasized? Underemphasized?

6. Under what circumstances do you think anointing is appropriate?

7. Is anointing appropriate in end-of-life situations when recovery is either unlikely or even not desired?

8. Reflect on those occasions when you have felt an anointing would have been appropriate but you felt uncomfortable asking for an anointing, or asking another if they would like to be anointed. If possible, share these with the group.

Additional Questions Regarding The Laying On Of Hands And Public Prayer

1. List those events in the life of the church that represent a significant transition in the life of an individual. Which of those, do you think, calls for the laying on of hands and public prayer?

2. Are you comfortable with others laying hands upon you? Under what circumstances would some people feel more comfortable than others in the laying on of hands?

3. In what circumstances have you witnessed or participated in public prayer for an individual, either in worship or in small group? What is your earliest memory about the matter? What were your feelings at that time? What are your feelings now about the event?

4. If individuals are uncomfortable with prayer before the entire congregation, how can the church pray with, and for, those who may benefit from this blessing in a manner that is comfortable for them?

Experiential Exercises

1. Arrange to look up an article on anointing on the internet, in a church book or manual, or in *The Brethren Encyclopedia*. Consider setting up a time of anointing for your small group.

2. Discuss the possibilities of arranging one Sunday a month for anointing. Discuss with leaders the possibility of a special sermon on the place of anointing in the life of the Brethren and in your congregation.

Children's Activity

Olive oil is at the heart of the anointing service, and that oil comes, of course, from olives and olive trees. Olive trees are more than just trees in the Middle East. They are considered a part of the family. Olive trees may live as long as 1,000 years and they are a legacy that is passed from generation to generation.

Many people make claims about olive oil and its place in a healthy diet. As you spend time with young people on the topic of anointing, take time to learn about olives and olive oil, as well. (Note that three of these involve some kind of eating and work equally well for younger and older believers!)

Here are some possible activities:

1. Take time to research olive trees and olive oil on the internet. Supervise the group as a search engine is used to find suitable websites.

2. Make your own croutons, baking bread cubes, or use the soft bread cubes without baking them. Lay out little cups of olive oil, sprinkling in a little oregano and basil. Using toothpicks, dip bread into oil, then eat.

3. Bake real garlic bread by slicing loaves of Italian or French bread lengthwise, brushing olive oil on the bread, then sprinkling a little oregano, basil, garlic powder, and parmesan cheese on the slices. Broil until lightly toasted.

4. Here's my favorite recipe involving olive oil. Sauté garlic, two sliced onions, and several green, yellow, and sweet red peppers in olive oil. Stir in a large can of tomato paste along with chili powder, oregano, and basil, pour into a glass dish, sprinkle cheese over everything, cover with lid, and bake for 45 minutes at 300 degrees. Lead a session while it's cooking and serve up the treat afterward.

Brethren Resources

There are some resources available through Brethren Press, the publishing arm of the Church of the Brethren that discuss the matter of anointing. You may be aware of other resources in your own traditions and communions.

Journey in Jesus' Way Video (produced by David Sollenberger)
Deacon Manual for Caring Ministries
For All Who Minister
The Brethren Encyclopedia